GUITAR

Audio
Access
Included

PLAYBACK+
Speed • Pitch • Balance • Loop

Russ
BARENBERG
T E A C H E S
20 Bluegrass Guitar Solos
Repertoire Tunes for
Intermediate Players

T0045357

To access audio online, visit:
www.halleonard.com/mylibrary

Enter Code
7663-9191-1246-7928

Cover Photo by Adam Traum

Audio Editor: Ted Orr

Mastered by: Ted Orr at
Nevessa Productions, Woodstock, NY

Produced by Happy Traum for Homespun Tapes

ISBN 978-0-7935-8335-5

EXCLUSIVELY DISTRIBUTED BY

7777 W. BLUEMOUND RD. P.O. BOX 13819 MILWAUKEE, WI 53213

Visit Hal Leonard Online at **www.halleonard.com**

Visit Homespun Tapes on the internet at **www.homespun.com**

GUITAR **Listen & Learn**
HOMESPUN MUSIC INSTRUCTION

Russ BARENBERG
TEACHES
20 Bluegrass Guitar Solos
Repertoire Tunes for Intermediate Players

Table of Contents

Discography

The following is a brief listing of good performances of some of the songs taught in this book. It is not by any means a complete discography, as most of this material has been recorded dozens of times by many great groups through the years. Use this as a guide, and try to seek out other versions on your own.

"John Henry"
Kentucky Colonels, *Appalachian Swing* (United Artists)

"Hot Corn, Cold Corn"
Flatt and Scruggs at Carnegie Hall (Columbia) also
David Grisman, Herb Pederson, et al., *Here Today* (Rounder 0169)

"Blackberry Blossom"
Sonny Miller, fiddle, *Virginia Breakdown* (County 705) also
Mark O'Connor, *Markology* (Rounder 0090)

"Leather Britches"
Hot Rize, *Traditional Ties* (Sugar Hill 3748) also
Sam Bush (with Norman Blake) *Late As Usual* (Rounder 0195)

"Whitesburg"
Fiddle Fever, *Waltz Of The Wind* (Flying Fish 303)

"Molly And Tenbrooks"
Bill Monroe, *The Original Bluegrass Sound* (Columbia) also
The Bluegrass Album (Rounder 0140)

"John Hardy"
Tony Rice, *Cold On The Shoulder* (Rounder 0183)

*The user should note there are slight variations between the fast and slow versions of these songs. All music has been approved by Russ Barenberg.

◆ Liberty

Capo II

w/ Example 2, 2nd time

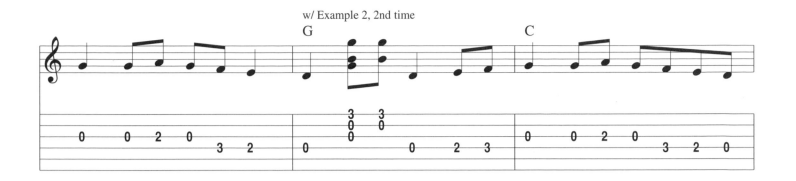

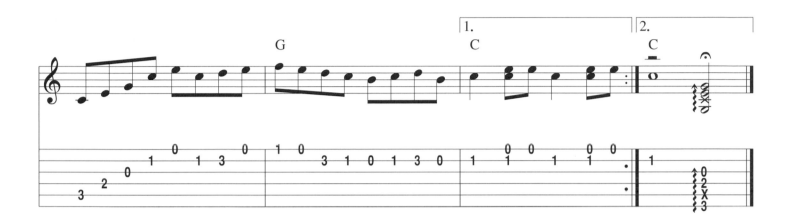

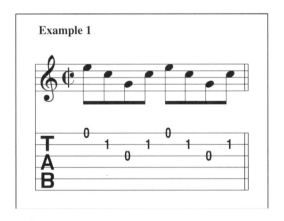

Example 1

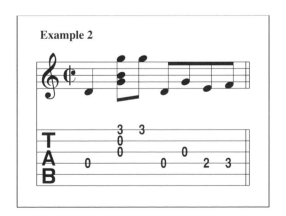

Example 2

◆ 8 Soldier's Joy

Capo II

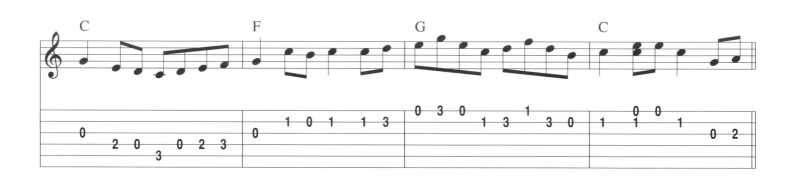

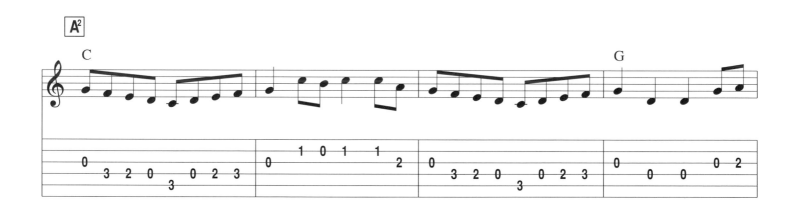

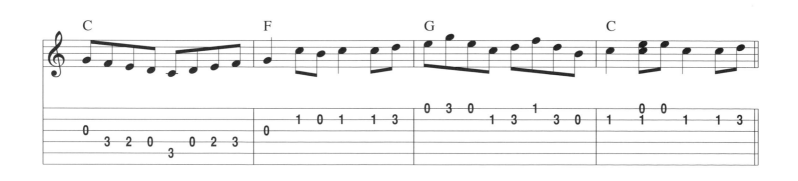

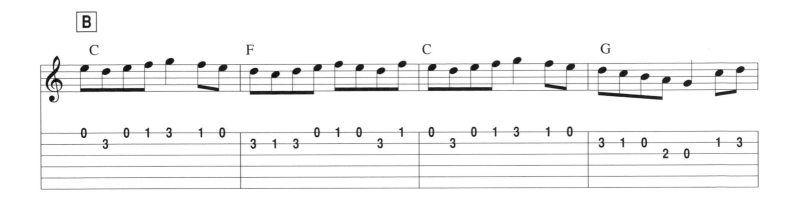

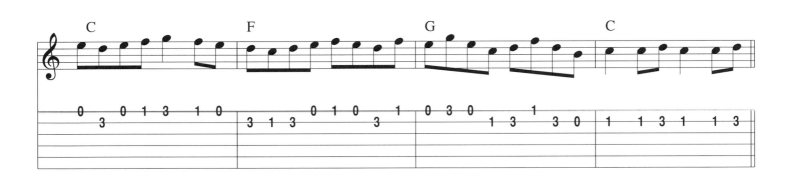

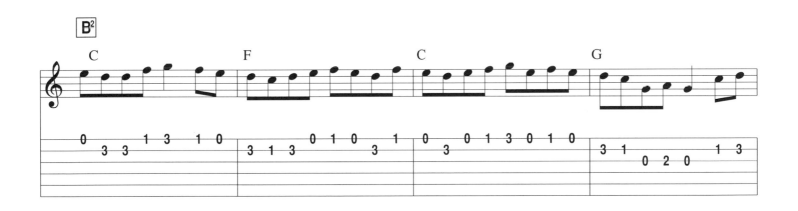

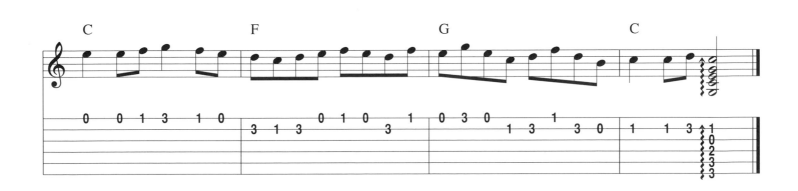

🎵 Little Annie

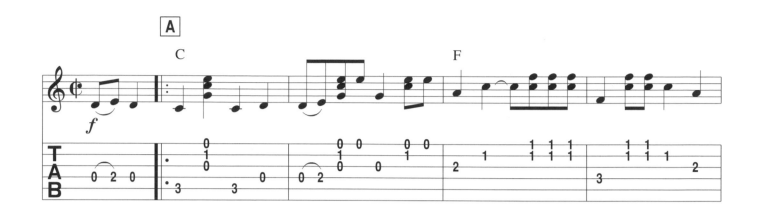

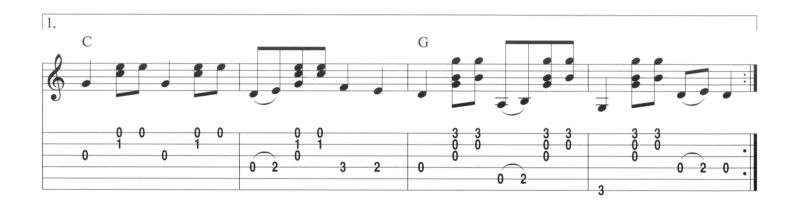

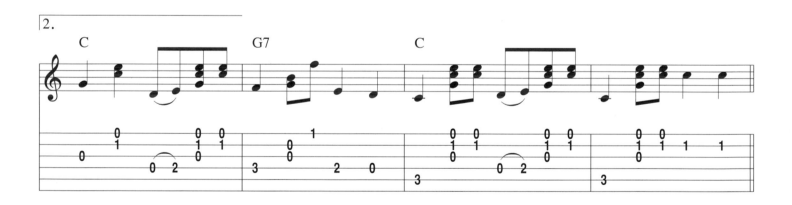

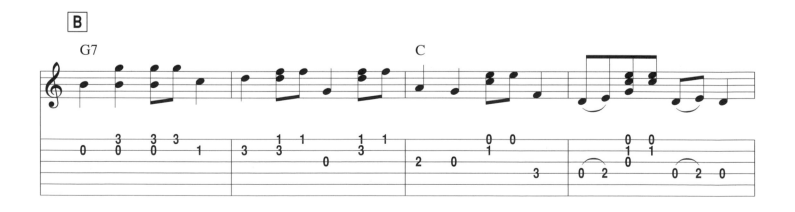

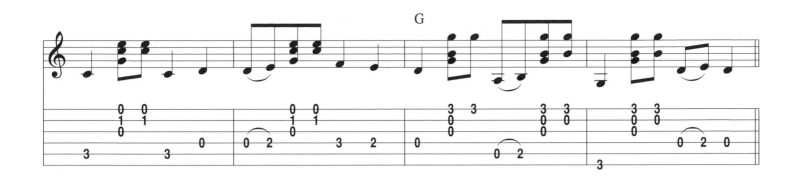

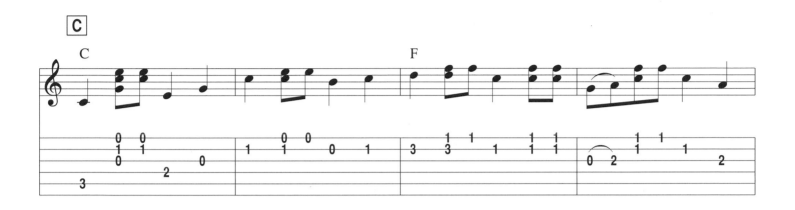

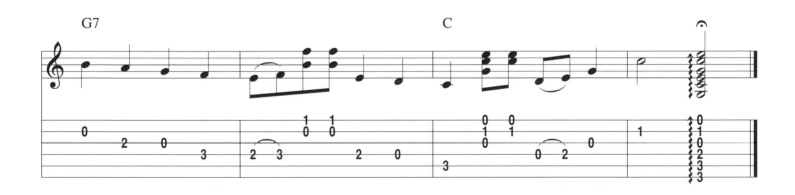

◆15 The Eighth of January

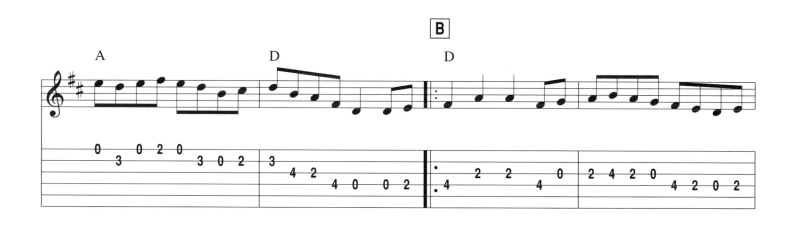

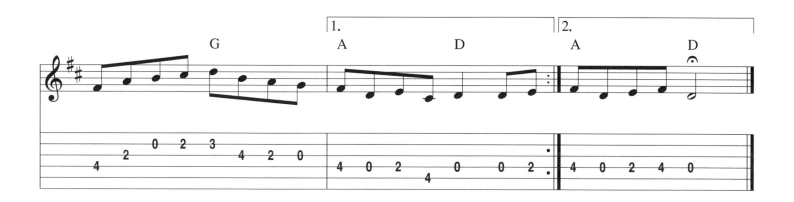

18 John Henry

22 Hot Corn, Cold Corn

Capo IV

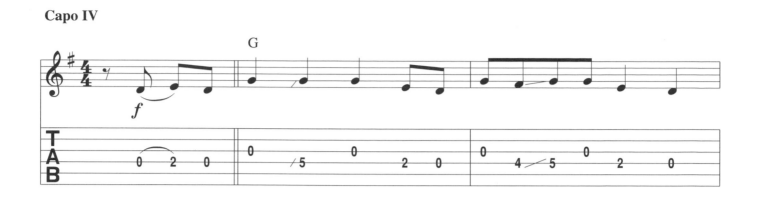

26 Blackberry Blossom

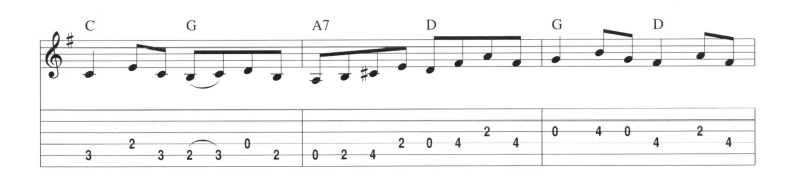

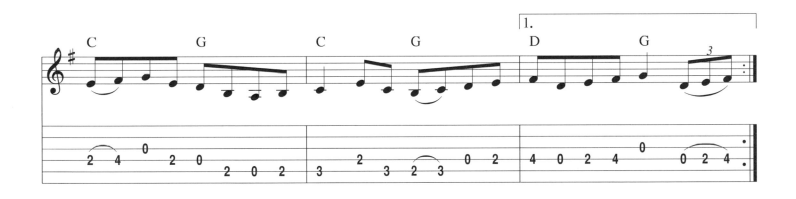

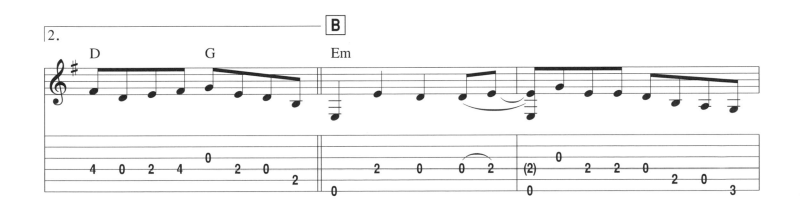

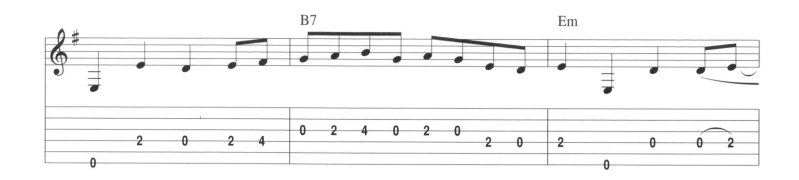

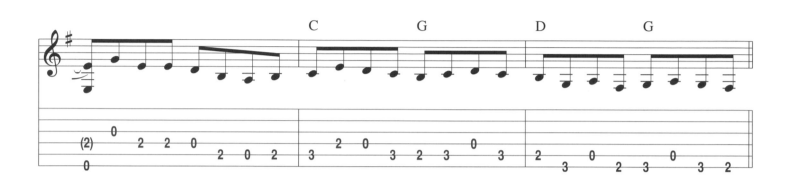

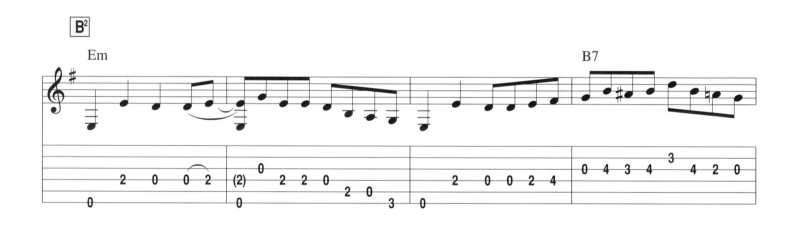

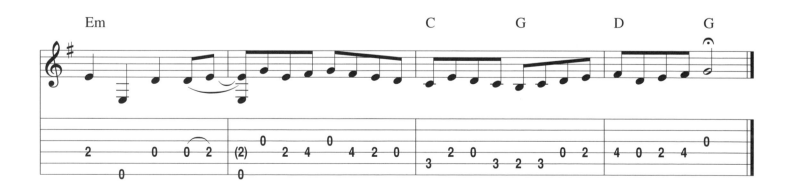

29 ◆ Down Yonder

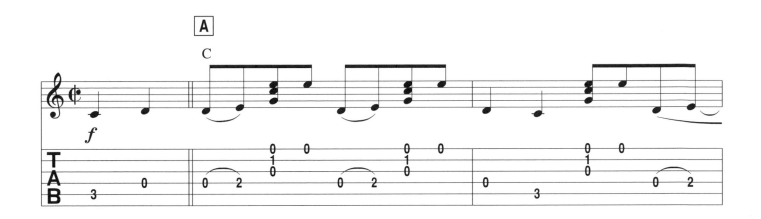

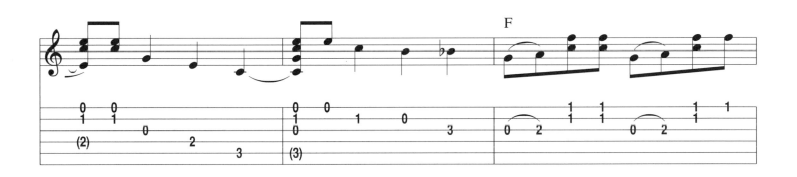

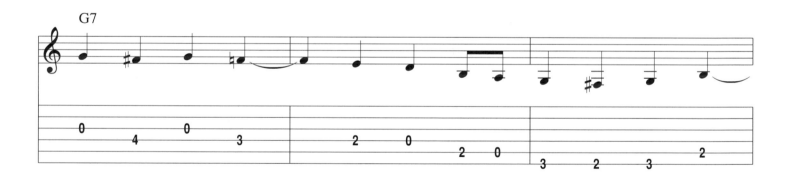

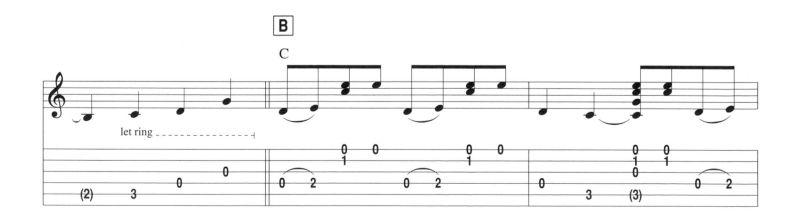

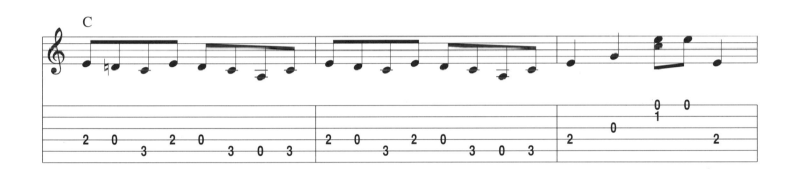

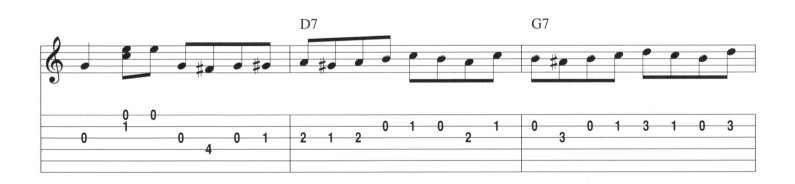

33 Leather Britches

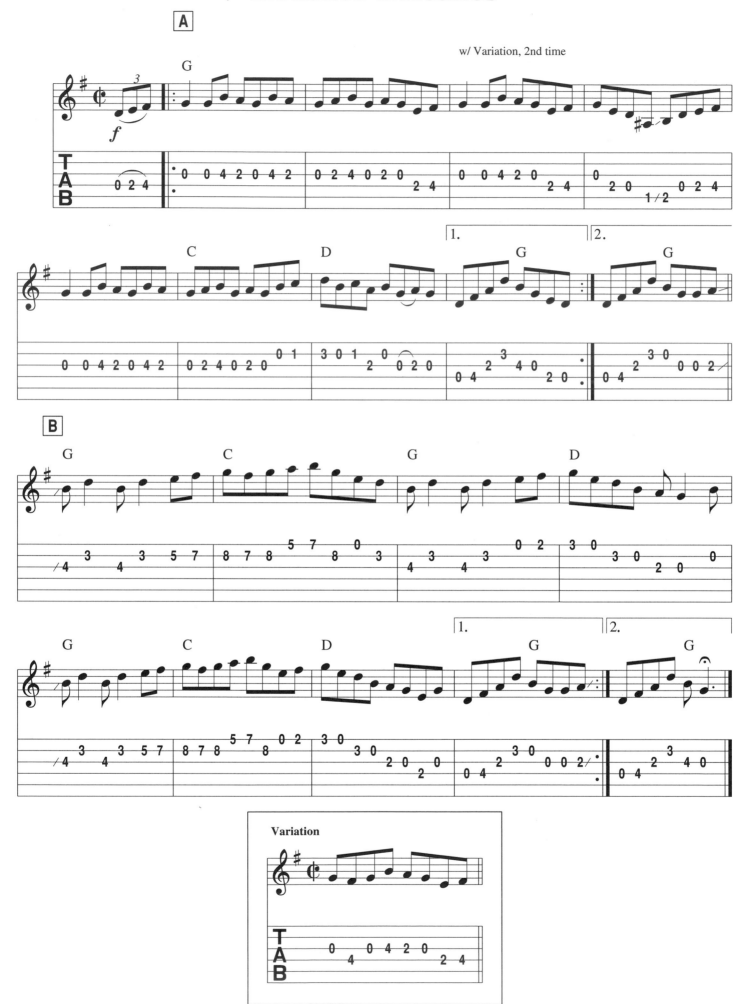

Whitesburg

(High Register)

Capo II

◆40 Whitesburg

(Low Register)

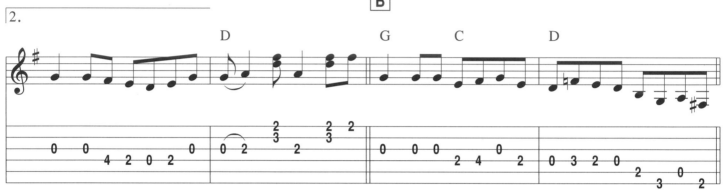

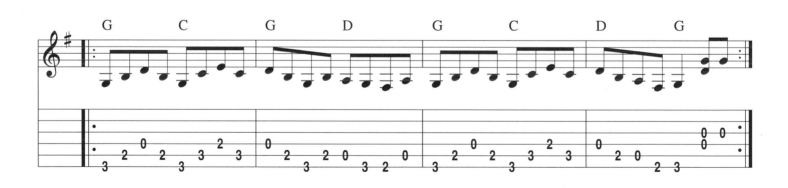

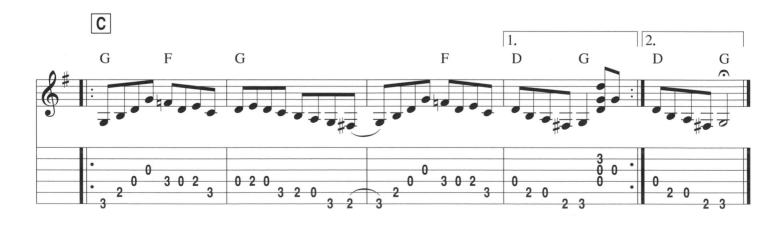

◆43 Molly and Tenbrooks

Capo IV

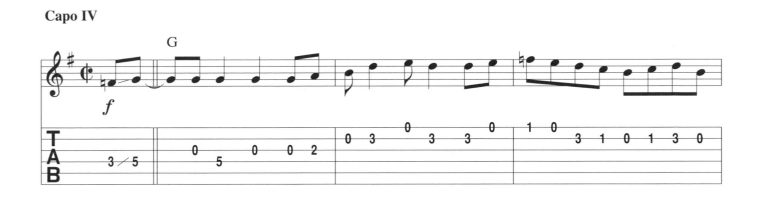

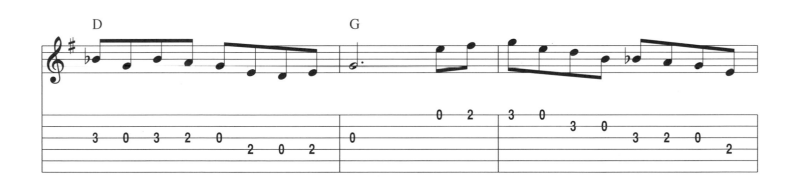

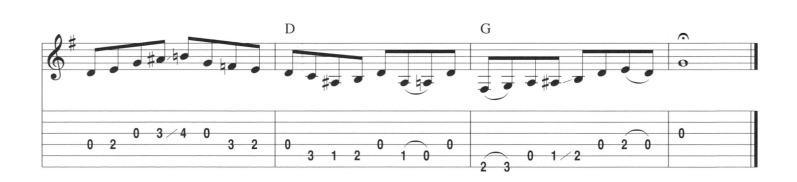

48 John Hardy

51 Fisher's Hornpipe

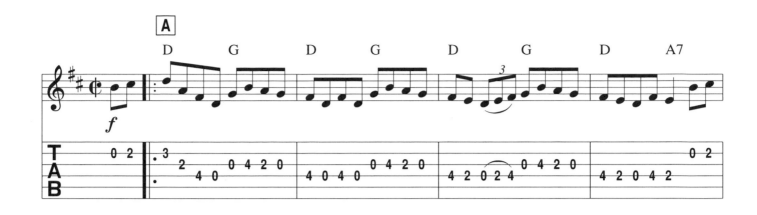

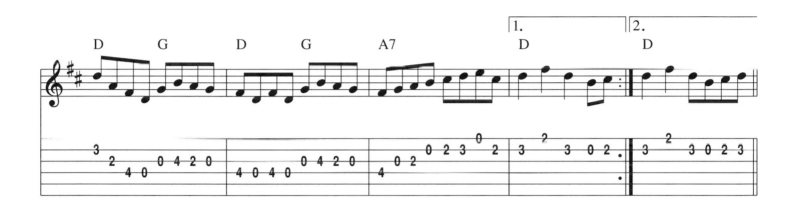

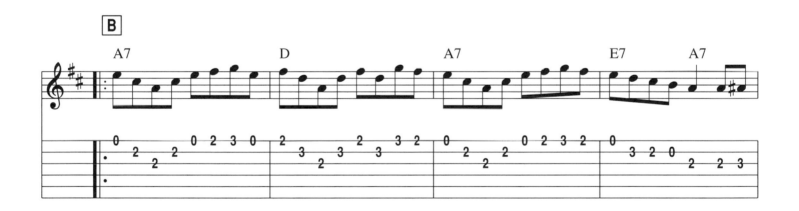

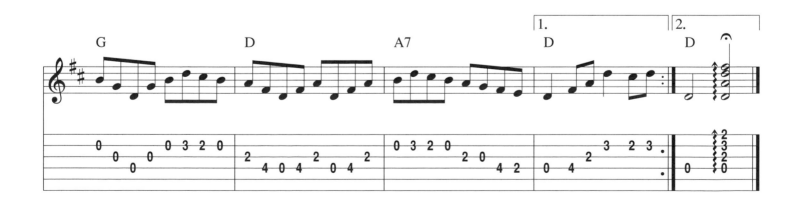

🔷 55 Forked Deer

59 ◆ Opera Reel

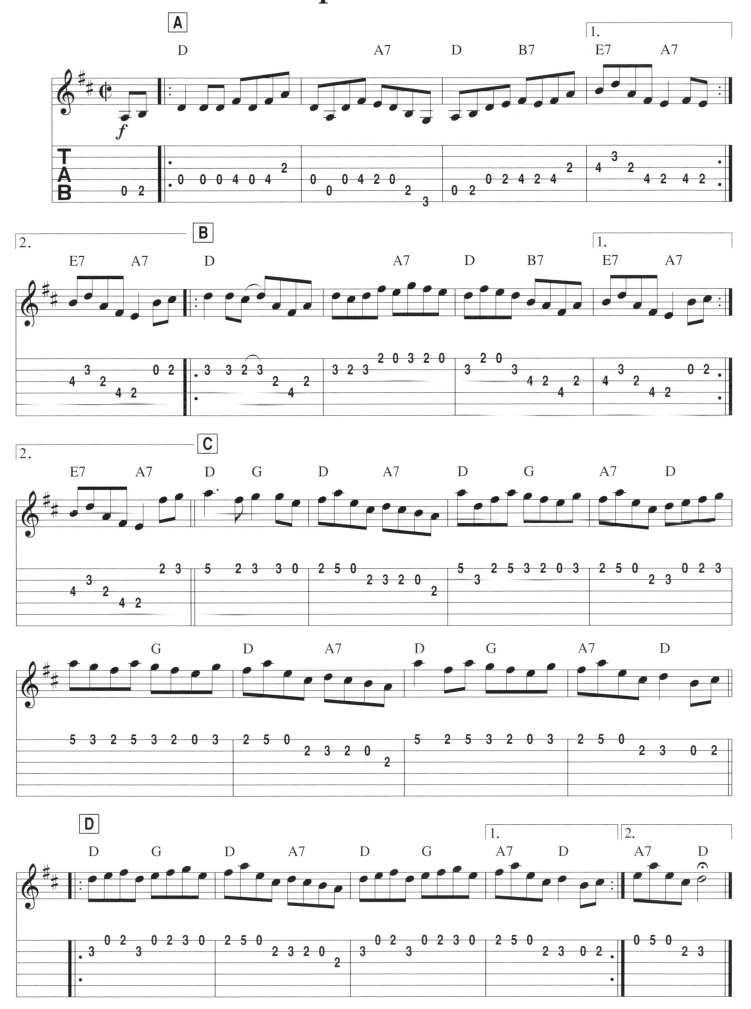

◆61 Temperance Reel

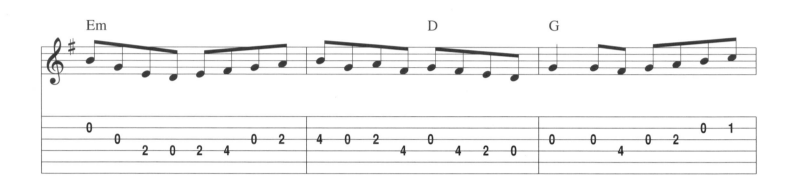

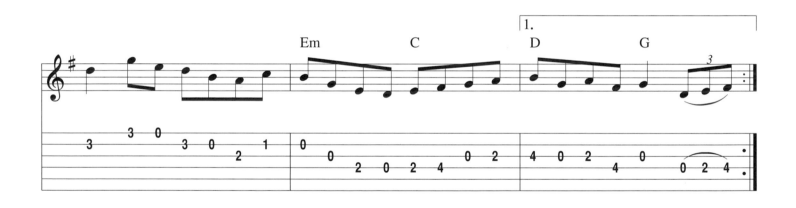

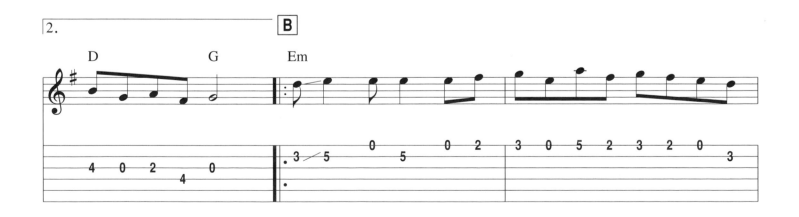

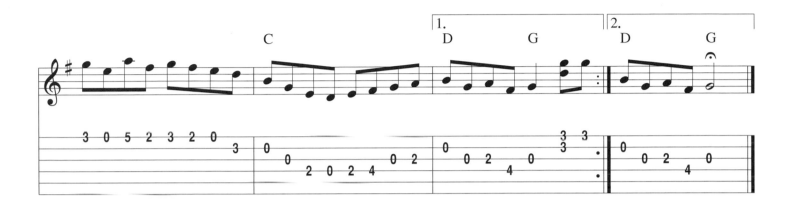

Note: The following progression is used to accompany the repeat of B .

St. Anne's Reel

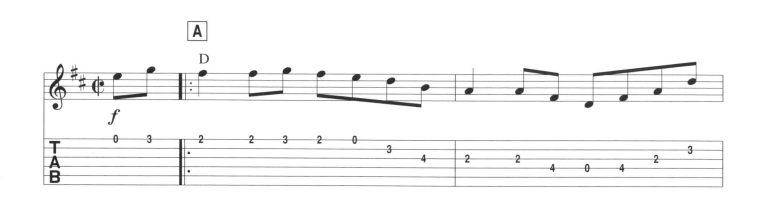

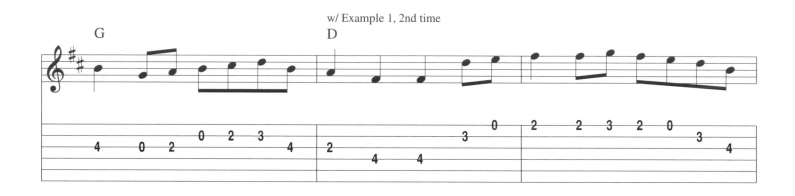

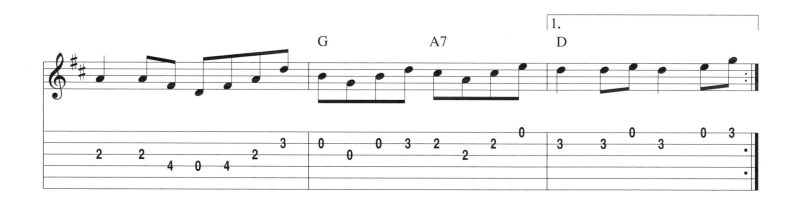

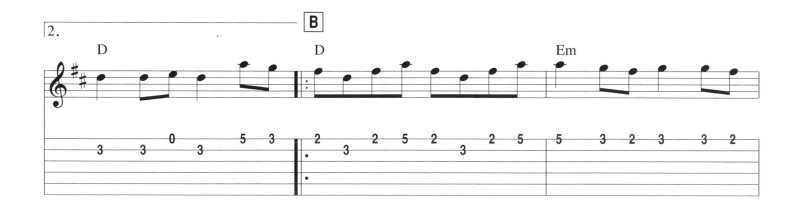

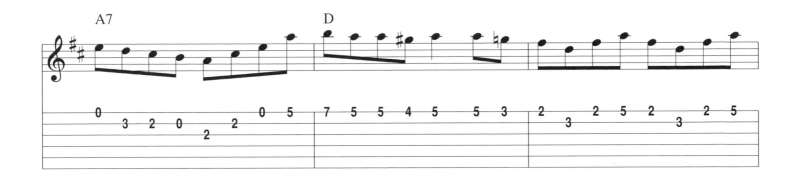

Example 1

🔷67 Red-Haired Boy

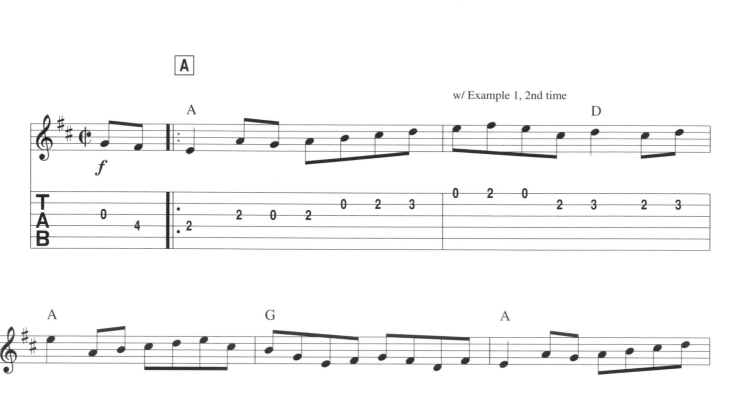

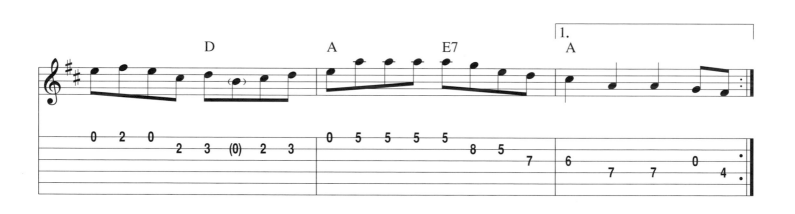

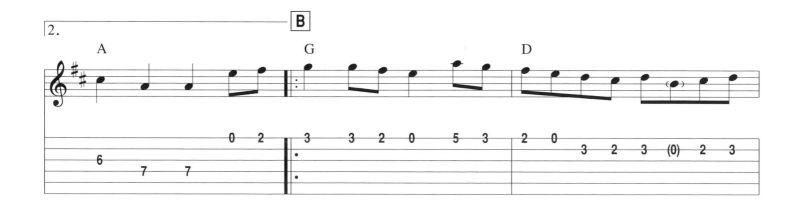

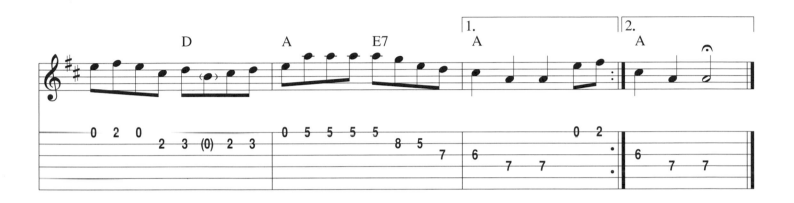

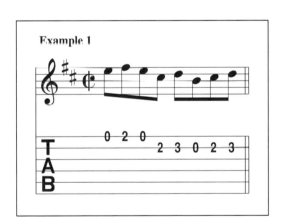

Example 1

MORE GREAT GUITAR TITLES FROM

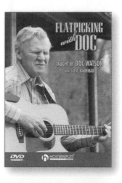

ALL STAR BLUEGRASS JAM ALONG

BACKUPS, LEAD PARTS AND NOTE-FOR-NOTE TRANSCRIPTIONS FOR 21 ESSENTIAL TUNES
featuring David Grier

These fabulous collections for players of all levels feature 21 must-know bluegrass songs & instrumentals, created especially for learning players by the genre's leading artists. The CD provides the audio versions of the solos, plus multiple rhythm tracks performed at moderate tempo for easy play-along.
00641943 Book/CD Pack $19.95

BEYOND BASIC BLUEGRASS RHYTHM GUITAR

BACKUP TECHNIQUES FOR INTERMEDIATE AND ADVANCED PLAYERS
Taught by Steve Kaufman

Flatpicking master teacher Steve Kaufman takes rhythm playing to a whole new level with this in-depth lesson. He covers chord substitutions, walking bass lines, complex chord shapes, and accompaniment ideas for a variety of tunes.
00642090 DVD $29.95 **TAB** **DVD**

NORMAN BLAKE'S GUITAR TECHNIQUES

taught by Norman Blake

Legendary guitarist Norman Blake teaches flatpicking fundamentals and a variety of bluegrass and old-time country guitar techniques.
00641613 2-DVD Set $49.95 **DVD**

BLUEGRASS GUITAR BUNDLE PACK

This budget-saving bundle pack includes *All Star Bluegrass Jam Along for Guitar* book/CD pack and *Bluegrass Guitar* DVD.
Early intermediate level.
00123272 Book/CD/DVD Pack $44.95 **TAB** **DVD**

THE CARTER FAMILY BUNDLE PACK

Bundle and save with this special pack that includes *The Carter Family Collection* book and the *Guitar Styles of the Carter Family* DVD. Beginner level.
00123284 Book/DVD Pack $44.95 **TAB** **DVD**

EARLY SOUTHERN GUITAR STYLES

taught by Mike Seeger

Mike Seeger, arguably our nation's most knowledgeable performer of American traditional music, teaches a wide variety of guitar techniques that were played in the rural South from about 1850 to 1930. He covers 25 songs and accompaniments, demonstrating each of them on a vintage instrument.
00642080 Two DVDs $39.95 **TAB** **DVD**

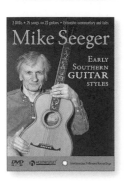

FLATPICKING WITH DOC

taught by Doc Watson

This unique lesson with the incomparable Doc Watson provides detailed instruction for thirteen of his most popular songs and instrumentals
00641621 DVD $39.95 **DVD**

GET STARTED ON BLUEGRASS AND COUNTRY GUITAR!

A COMPLETE LESSON FOR BEGINNERS
Taught by Steve Kaufman

Steve Kaufman introduces new players to all the elements of guitar flatpicking. No previous experience is necessary. All that's needed is a guitar, a flatpick and the desire to accompany and play lead on great folk, bluegrass and country songs.
00642158 DVD $29.95 **TAB** **DVD**

GREAT GUITAR LESSONS – BLUEGRASS FLATPICKING

by Russ Barenberg, Norman Blake, Dan Crary, Nick Forster, Steve Kaufman, Tony Rice, Happy Traum

These lessons for both novices and advanced pickers in flatpick style will help guitarists play the notes and make music out of them as well. Seven celebrated bluegrass artists tackle everything from simple backup to hot bluegrass solos.
00641990 DVD $24.95 **TAB** **DVD**

TONY RICE – GUITAR BUNDLE PACK

TONY RICE TEACHES BLUEGRASS GUITAR

Includes the book/CD pack *Tony Rice Teaches Bluegrass Guitar* and the DVD *Tony Rice – Master Class* in one money-saving pack!
00642056 Book/CD/DVD Pack $44.95 **DVD**

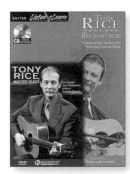

BRYAN SUTTON'S SECRETS FOR SUCCESSFUL FLATPICKING

taught by Bryan Sutton

One of bluegrass and country music's most high-profile acoustic guitarists lays out his tricks of the trade for aspiring players. This extraordinary DVD is filled with spectacular picking, detailed instruction and invaluable advice.
00641997 DVD $29.95 **DVD**

HAPPY TRAUM BLUEGRASS PACK

Includes the book/CD *Bluegrass Guitar* and the DVD *Easy Bluegrass and Country Guitar*, in one convenient pack!
00642131 Book/CD/DVD Pack $39.95 **TAB** **DVD**

FOR MORE INFORMATION, SEE YOUR LOCAL MUSIC DEALER, OR WRITE TO:

HAL•LEONARD® CORPORATION
7777 W. BLUEMOUND RD. P.O. BOX 13819 MILWAUKEE, WI 53213

www.halleonard.com

Prices, contents, and availability subject to change without notice.

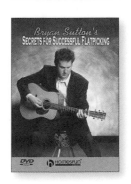

0416